D1406190

Meet
Paul Revere
Revolutionary Hero

Enslow Publishing
101 W. 23rd Street
Suite 240
New York, NY 10011
USA

enslow.com

Jane Katirgis and Rose McCarthy

Published in 2020 by Enslow Publishing, LLC
101 W. 23rd Street, Suite 240, New York, NY 10011

Library of Congress Cataloging-in-Publication Data

Names: Katirgis, Jane, author. | McCarthy, Rose, author.
Title: Meet Paul Revere : revolutionary hero / Jane Katirgis and Rose McCarthy.
Description: New York : Enslow Publishing, 2020 | Series: Introducing famous Americans | Includes bibliographical references and index. | Audience: Grades 3–5.
Identifiers: LCCN 2018060043 | ISBN 9781978511323 (library bound) | ISBN 9781978511309 (pbk.) | ISBN 9781978511316 (6 pack)
Subjects: LCSH: Revere, Paul, 1735–1818—Juvenile literature. | Statesmen—Massachusetts—Biography—Juvenile literature. | Massachusetts—Biography—Juvenile literature. | Massachusetts—History—Revolution, 1775–1783—Juvenile literature.
Classification: LCC F69.R43 K38 2020 | DDC 973.3/311092 [B]—dc23
LC record available at https://lccn.loc.gov/2018060043

Printed in the United States of America

To Our Readers: We have done our best to make sure all website addresses in this book were active and appropriate when we went to press. However, the author and the publisher have no control over and assume no liability for the material available on those websites or on any websites they may link to. Any comments or suggestions can be sent by email to customerservice@enslow.com.

Portions of this book originally appeared in *Paul Revere: Freedom Rider.*

Contents

1 Young Paul Revere

In 1775, the British army was set to attack the American colonies. Paul Revere's famous ride helped warn the colonists. Revere also helped the American colonies become the United States of America. But there's a lot more to know about Paul Revere. He was a brave and talented patriot.

This early 1800s painting of Paul Revere was done in watercolor on ivory.

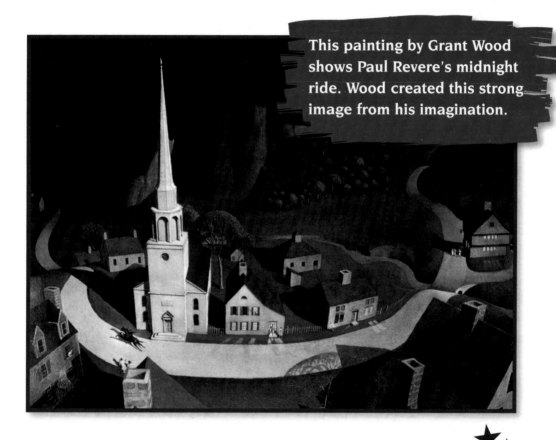

This painting by Grant Wood shows Paul Revere's midnight ride. Wood created this strong image from his imagination.

Let's Learn More

Paul was also a bell ringer at church. One evening a week, he rang bells for two hours. Bells could weigh almost a ton. Ringing bells was hard work!

Paul was born in Boston in 1735. Boston was in the colony of Massachusetts. His father, a French immigrant, was a silversmith. When Paul was about 13 years old, he became his father's apprentice.

In 1754, Paul's father died. Paul took over the family business. He married Sarah Orne in 1757.

Paul Revere also worked as a dentist. This 1768 ad from the *Boston Gazette* instructs patients to call on Revere if they have any loose teeth.

and it is not unlikely to be an armed Cutter bound hither, one or two of them being daily expected.

WHEREAS many Persons are so unfortunate as to lose their Fore-Teeth by Accident, and otherways; to their great Detriment, not only in Looks, but speaking both in Public and Private :—This is to inform all such, that they may have them re-placed with artificial Ones, that looks as well as the Natural, & answers the End of Speaking to all Intents, by *PAUL REVERE*, Goldsmith, near the Head of Dr. *Clarke*'s Wharf, *Boston*.

. All Persons who have had false Teeth fixt by Mr. *John Baker*, Surgeon-Dentist, and they have got loose (as they will in Time) may have them fastened by the above, who learnt the Method of fixing them from Mr. *Baker*.

Boston, Printed by EDES & GILL,

The Sons of Liberty

2

Paul Revere was one of the people to start a group called the Sons of Liberty in 1765. The British ruled the American colonies. The colonists hated British taxes and unfair acts. The British called them rebels. The Sons of Liberty considered themselves patriots.

In 1770, British soldiers fired at rowdy colonists. Five people were killed. This event was called the Boston Massacre.

Let's Learn More

Paul also worked as a copper engraver. He created a famous image of the Boston Massacre.

Paul Revere copied a drawing by Henry Pelham of the 1770 Boston Massacre. He made this engraving. Revere's picture was printed first, making Pelham angry.

Paul's wife, Sarah, died in 1773. She had just given birth to her eighth child. Paul soon married Rachel Walker.

That same year, the British set a high tax on tea. Paul Revere and the Sons of Liberty staged the Boston Tea Party. Many of the men dressed up as Native Americans. They dumped boxes of British tea into Boston Harbor.

ADVERTISEMENT.

THE Members of the Aſſociation of the Sons of Liberty, are requeſted to meet at the City-Hall, at one o'Clock, To-morrow, (being Friday) on Buſineſs of the utmoſt Importance;—And every other Friend to the Liberties, and Trade of America, are hereby moſt cordially invited, to meet at the ſame Time and Place. *The Committee of the Aſſociation.*

Thurſday, NEW-YORK, 16th December, 1773.

This newspaper notice announces a group meeting held at City Hall in New York in 1773. The Sons of Liberty were American patriots.

The name of this drawing is *Liberty Triumphant; or the Downfall of Oppression*. A modern way to say the same thing is "Freedom wins; we won't be held down."

During 1773, Paul also carried messages to patriot leaders in other cities. He rode as far as New York and Maine.

Minutemen began to train in many towns. They had to be ready to fight the British at a minute's notice.

Many colonists became patriots. Some did not.

Let's Learn More

American towns had militias, or organized groups of colonists trained as soldiers. Minutemen were a select group of militiamen—often the younger, stronger, and quicker ones.

Laſt Wedneſday Night died, *Patrick Carr*, an Inhabitant of this Town, of the Wound he received in King-Street on the bloody and execrable Night of the 5th Inſtant——He had juſt before left his Home, and upon his coming into the Street received the fatal Ball in his Hip which paſſed out at the oppoſite Side ; this is the fifth Life that has been ſacrificed by the Rage of the Soldiery, but it is feared it will not be the laſt, as ſeveral others are dangerouſly languiſhing of their Wounds. His Remains were attended on Saturday laſt from Faneuil-Hall by a numerous and reſpectable Train of Mourners, to the *ſame* Grave, in which thoſe who fell by the *ſame* Hands of Violence were interred the laſt Week.

Paul Revere engraved and published Patrick Carr's death notice. British soldiers killed Carr, a colonist, in 1770 outside of his home during the Boston Massacre.

③ Revere's Ride

In April 1775, two patriot leaders were staying in Lexington, Massachusetts. They were Samuel Adams and John Hancock. The patriots realized that the British would soon attack. Patriots stored arms and supplies in nearby Concord.

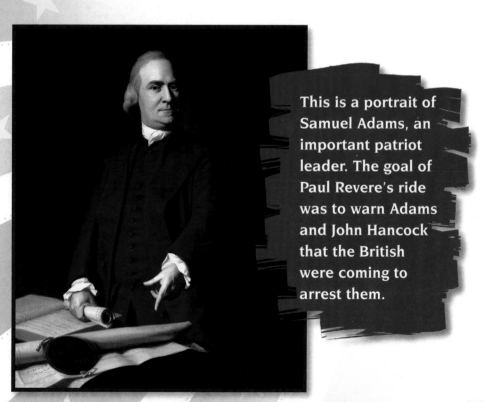

This is a portrait of Samuel Adams, an important patriot leader. The goal of Paul Revere's ride was to warn Adams and John Hancock that the British were coming to arrest them.

On April 18, the British had assembled. Patriot leaders asked Paul to spread the news. Paul Revere began his midnight ride.

Paul went to Christ Church. He told friends to hang two lamps in the steeple. This sent a signal to nearby Charlestown. It meant that the British would come by sea. Paul sneaked across the river in a boat.

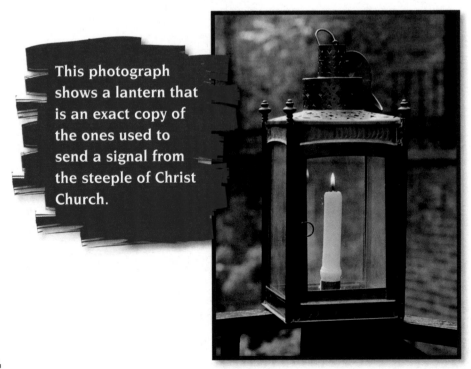

This photograph shows a lantern that is an exact copy of the ones used to send a signal from the steeple of Christ Church.

Paul borrowed a horse and rode to Lexington. British patrols tried to stop him. Paul outran them. He spread the alarm to every house he passed. When he reached Lexington, he alerted Adams and Hancock.

The British captured Paul as he headed to Concord. But another rider escaped to spread the warning. Paul was soon released.

This is another painting of Paul Revere's ride near Boston.

Let's Learn More

Paul helped spy on the British. He and other patriots patrolled the streets at night watching the British soldiers.

Paul Revere wrote about his work carrying messages in this 1798 letter. He wrote that one of the men who worked with him was probably a British spy.

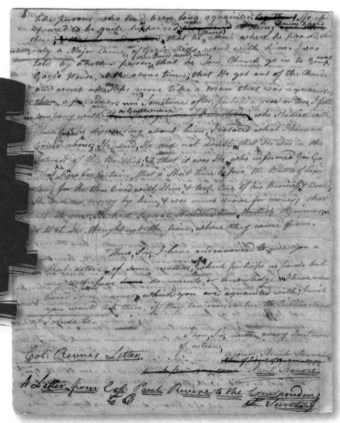

Battling the British

4

Paul Revere's warning helped prepare the militiamen of Lexington. About 70 men met the British army of over 600. The British tried to pass. Someone fired a musket. Nobody knows who shot first. The two sides exchanged fire. The militiamen fell back. The British marched toward Concord.

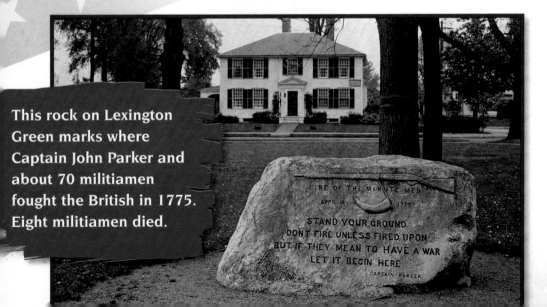

This rock on Lexington Green marks where Captain John Parker and about 70 militiamen fought the British in 1775. Eight militiamen died.

The colored lines show the paths taken by riders on the night of Paul Revere's famous ride. The red path shows Revere's route. William Dawes (blue) and Samuel Prescott (orange) were the other messengers.

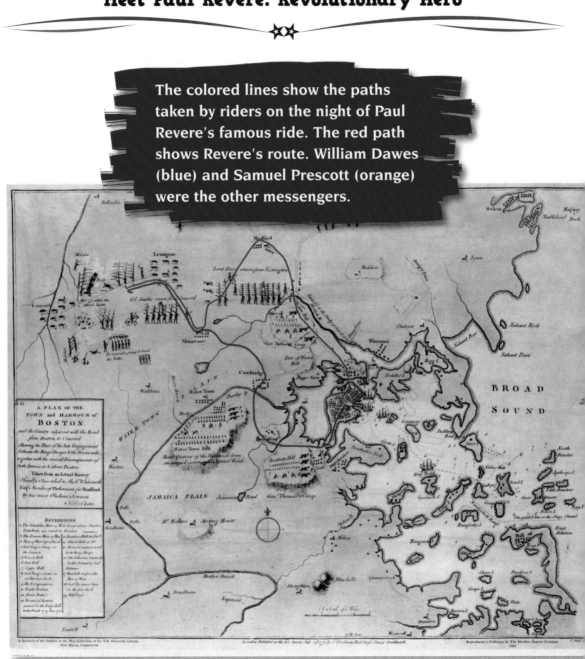

Hundreds of militiamen waited for the British at Concord. The two sides battled at the North Bridge.

The British marched back to Lexington. The militiamen continued to fire at them from the sides of the road. That road is now known as Battle Road.

Let's Learn More

News of the Battle of Lexington and Concord travelled quickly around the American colonies. However, the Americans would not declare their independence until over a year later.

As British troops retreated to Boston, the militiamen attacked them. It was a major victory for the militiamen.

The Revolutionary War had begun. Paul joined the army. Many soldiers died. Paul was expelled because he did not follow orders. Later he cleared his name.

Let's Learn More

A poem by Henry Wadsworth Longfellow helped turn Paul into a folk hero. It begins with these words:

> Listen, my children, and you shall hear
> Of the midnight ride of Paul Revere.
> On the eighteenth of April, in Seventy-Five:
> Hardly a man is now alive
> Who remembers that famous day and year.

In this picture by Amos Doolittle, the British army is marching back to Boston. They have just met the patriot army at Lexington and Concord. People who had seen this event told the artist what had happened.

Left: The gravestone of William French, shot in Vermont by a British officer a month before the Battle of Lexington and Concord. At age 22, he was the first patriot killed in the War for Independence. *Below*: In 1775, patriot soldiers hid behind the stone walls and trees on this road and shot British soldiers. The British were retreating to Boston after the battle at Concord.

Paul Revere's Later Life

5

In 1783, the Revolutionary War ended. Paul applied himself to his business and family. The silversmith shop made more money than ever. His eleven children grew up.

He branched out in business. He opened a foundry. It produced small metal parts for ships, such as spikes and nails. It also made huge bells.

Paul Revere owned a copper rolling mill, where he made bolts, nails, and spikes. These were used to build a ship called the USS *New Hampshire* in 1819.

In 1773, Paul Revere crafted this silver tea service. Dr. William Paine ordered it as a gift for his bride.

✫✫

When Paul was 66 years old, he opened a copper mill. The navy used Paul's copper to make the bottoms of ships.

Rachel Revere died in 1813. Paul passed away in 1818. The country mourned a great patriot. Today we honor Paul as a true American hero.

Paul Revere owned a foundry with his son. This card advertises the business. Workers at the foundry made bells, cannons, nails, and other metal objects.

PAUL REVERE and SON, Foundry at the North part of BOSTON. at their Bell and Cannon Cast Bells and Brass Cannon of all Sizes, and all kinds of Composition Work. Manufacture Sheets, Bolts, Spikes, Nails, &c. from Malleable Copper and Cold Rolled. NB Cash for Old Brass & Copper.

Revere. 1801.

201.

This engraving of Paul Revere was done in 1801 when he was 66 years old.

Timeline

1735—Paul Revere is born in Boston.

1757—Paul marries Sarah Orne.

1765—The Sons of Liberty begin meeting.

1770—The Boston Massacre takes place.

1773—Paul's wife, Sarah, dies. Paul marries Rachel Walker. The Boston Tea Party occurs on December 16.

1775—Paul makes his midnight ride on April 18. The Battle of Lexington and Concord occurs on April 19.

1783—The Revolutionary War ends.

1813—Paul's second wife, Rachel, dies.

1818—Paul dies in Boston.

Glossary

apprentice (uh-PREN-tis) A person who learns a trade by working for an experienced person.

assemble (uh-SEM-bull) To gather together.

engraver (en-GRAYV-ur) One who carves, cuts, or etches into a block or surface used for printing.

foundry (FOUN-dree) A place where metal is melted and shaped.

immigrant (IH-muh-grint) Someone who moves to a new country from another country.

massacre (MA-sih-ker) The act of killing a large number of people or animals.

minutemen (MIH-nuht-men) Armed Americans who were ready to fight the British at a moment 's notice.

patriot (PAY-tree-uht) Someone who loves his or her country and is prepared to fight for it.

rebel (REH-bul) A person who disobeys the people or country in charge.

silversmith (SIL-vur-smith) Someone who makes or repairs silver objects.

Learn More

Books

Doeden, Matt. *The Colonists Revolt: An Interactive American Revolution Adventure*. North Mankato, MN: Capstone Press, 2019.

Goddu, Krystyna Poray. *What's Your Story, Paul Revere?* Minneapolis, MN: Lerner Publications, 2016.

Kallio, Jamie. *12 Questions About Paul Revere's Ride*. Mankato, MN: 2-Story Library, 2016.

Websites

Paul Revere Biography
paulreverehouse.org/biography
Learn more details about Paul Revere's life and trade.

Paul Revere Biography, Facts, and Worksheets
kidskonnect.com/people/paul-revere/
Explore more about one of the most well-known people in the Revolutionary War.

The Real Story of Paul Revere's Ride
biography.com/news/paul-reveres-ride-facts
Read more information about Paul Revere's ride.

Primary Source Image List

Page 4: Portrait of Paul Revere, by Chester Harding, c. 1823. After Gilbert Stuart's 1813 portrait.

Page 6: Advertisement from the *Boston Gazette* dated September 19, 1768.

Page 8: *Bloody Massacre*, engraved in 1770 by Paul Revere after a drawing by Henry Pelham.

Page 9: Advertisement calling a meeting of the members of the association of the Sons of Liberty in New York City on December 16, 1773.

Page 10: *Liberty Triumphant, or The Downfall of Oppression*, 1773 engraving by Henry Dawkins.

Page 12: Obituary of Patrick Carr. March 5, 1770, broadside article engraved and published by Paul Revere.

Page 13: Portrait of Samuel Adams, by John Singleton Copley, oil on canvas, c. 1772.

Page 16: Letter from Colonel Paul Revere to Jeremy Belknap, 1798.

Page 18: A *plan of the town and harbor of Boston and the country adjacent*, engraved by Charles Hall and published in London by J. De Costa, July 29, 1775.

Page 21: *British Retreat to Boston*, engraved by Amos Doolittle from first-hand accounts.

★★

Page 23: Copper ship fittings manufactured c. 1819 by Paul Revere's copper rolling mill in Canton, Massachusetts, for the USS *New Hampshire*.

Page 24: "Paine Service" by Paul Revere in silver, 1773. Commissioned by Dr. William Paine for his bride, Lois Orne.

Page 25: Trade card for Paul Revere and Son engraved by Thomas Clarke between 1796 and 1803. This print was done in 1944.

Page 26: *Revere.* 1801, engraved by Charles Saint-Mémin.

Index